Bell Pepper Heaven on a Plate

Red, Orange, Yellow, and Green Delicious Bell Pepper Recipes

BY: Keanu Wood

Copyright © 2021 by Keanu Wood. All Rights Reserved.

License and Copyright

All rights reserved. This publication cannot be transmitted in any form. Whether parts or whole, distributed, or reproduced through any means, including recording, photocopying, or other media.

If you need to replicate any part of this content, you must seek permission from the author. Remember, the author will not be held responsible for your interpretation of the contents of this book. However, it is adequately researched to ensure all the contents are accurate.

Table of Contents

Introduction 5

(1) Sesame Cauliflower and Bell Pepper Skillet 7

(2) Asian Pork and Pepper Skillet 9

(3) Turkey and Quinoa Stuffed Peppers 11

(4) Unstuffed Turkey Bell Peppers 13

(5) Pork, Brown Rice and Olives Stuffed Peppers 15

(6) Roasted Pepper Salad with Balsamic Vinaigrette 17

(7) Sweet Pepper, Onion, and Mushroom Medley 19

(8) Cajun Chicken and Bell Pepper Bake 21

(9) Bell Pepper Eggs 23

(10) Peppers with Gnocchi and Sausage 25

(11) Gemelli in Roasted Pepper Sauce 27

(12) Buttered Steak with Peppers and Green Beans 29

(13) Chicken Fajita Peppers 31

(14) Chicken and Pepper Fusilli 34

(15) Italian Orzo Stuffed Bell Peppers 37

(16) Bell Pepper Nachos 39

(17) Lamb and Goat Cheese Stuffed Peppers 41

(18) Bell Pepper, Zucchini, and Snap Pea Stir-Fry 43

(19) Filet Mignon with Tarragon Peppers 46

(20) Rice and Chicken Stuffed Peppers 49

(21) Pesto Marinated Peppers 51

(22) Bell Pepper and Gorgonzola Bungalow 53

(23) Bell Pepper and Potato Ratatouille 55

(24) Mini Pizza Peppers 58

(25) Sweet Potato and Pepper Soup 60

(26) Curried Peppers and Potatoes 62

(27) Greek Stuffed Peppers 64

(28) Cajun Chicken Spaghetti with Peppers 66

(29) Herb Sautéed Green Peppers 69

(30) Peperonata 71

Afterthought 73

Biography 74

Introduction

We're not sure if you already love bell peppers or if you're only starting to incorporate them into your diet. Either way, this cookbook is perfect for you! Our recipes have been thought out for all level cooks who are looking to experiment a little with bell peppers in their kitchen. Why wouldn't you? They're crunchy, they're a little spicy, and a little bit sweet. They're the perfect pepper and this makes them extremely easy to cook with too!

You can sauté, bake, blend, and even boil them if you'd like! This is why they're so easy to add into most dishes, making your life easier. Bell Pepper Heaven on a Plate was written to help you navigate your way through the different colored peppers in all of your meals, hopefully making your weeknight dinners a lot more exciting and easy!

To help you get started, we've picked up a bunch of peppers from the supermarket and have already started to chop them up so you can throw them into the recipe of your choosing. If you're still unsure about what you can make with them, let us give you some ideas: sweet potato and pepper soup, peppers with gnocchi and sausage, fajitas, buttered steak with peppers, and ratatouille. These are some of the recipes we'll be teaching you how to make, so what will you start with? We're kind of hungry!

OOOOOOOOOOOOOOOOOOOOOOOOOOOOOOOOOO

(1) Sesame Cauliflower and Bell Pepper Skillet

Another exciting way to use bell peppers in a more loaded way. Cauliflower and bell peppers make a good pair for stir-fries.

Makes: 4

Preparation Time: 10 mins

Cooking Time: 15 mins

Ingredient List:

For sauce:

- 1 tablespoon rice vinegar
- 1 teaspoon grated fresh ginger
- 2 tablespoons hoisin sauce
- ¼ to ½ teaspoons red pepper flakes
- 1/3 cup soy sauce
- 2 garlic cloves, minced
- 1 teaspoon sesame oil
- 2 teaspoons cornstarch

For stir-fry:

- 2 tablespoons sesame oil
- 1 large cauliflower, cut into florets
- 1 large red bell pepper, seeds removed and cut into chunks
- 2 tablespoons chopped fresh scallions
- 1 tablespoon sesame seeds

oooooooooooooooooooooooooooooooo

How to Cook:

1. Combine all sauce ingredients in a bowl and set aside.

2. Heat sesame oil in a skillet and stir-fry cauliflower and bell pepper for 10 minutes or until tender.

3. Mix in sauce and simmer for 4 to 5 minutes. Stir in scallions and sesame seeds.

4. Dish stir-fry and serve with rice.

(2) Asian Pork and Pepper Skillet

Is your Chinese food craving up and loud? If you can't wait for delivery from your favorite Chinese restaurant, assemble this skillet quickly, pair it with rice, and satisfy that craving.

Makes: 4

Preparation Time: 10 mins

Cooking Time: 22 mins

Ingredient List:

- 1 tablespoon sesame oil
- Salt and black pepper to taste
- 1 large red bell pepper, seeds removed and sliced
- 1 large green bell pepper, seeds removed and sliced
- 1 large white onion, cut into chunks
- 4 boneless pork chops, cut into strips
- 2 garlic cloves, minced
- ¼ cup Shaoxing wine
- 1 teaspoon dark soy sauce, low sodium
- 1 teaspoon cornstarch

oooooooooooooooooooooooooooooooo

How to Cook:

1. Heat sesame oil in a large skillet, season pork with salt, black pepper, and cook in oil for 12 to 15 minutes or until cooked through. Transfer pork to a plate and set aside.

2. Add bell peppers and onion to skillet; sauté for 3 minutes or until sweaty and stir in garlic. Cook further for 1 minute or until fragrant.

3. In a bowl, mix Shaoxing wine, soy sauce, and cornstarch – return pork to skillet and top with sauce mixture. Combine well and simmer for 2 to 3 minutes or until slightly syrupy; adjust taste with salt and black pepper if necessary.

4. Dish food and serve warm with rice.

(3) Turkey and Quinoa Stuffed Peppers

Don't wait until Thanksgiving to enjoy turkey; here's a quick and easy way to include turkey in your weekly meals.

Makes: 4

Preparation Time: 10 mins

Cooking Time: 62 mins

Ingredient List:

- 1 tablespoon olive oil
- 1 lb. ground turkey
- 1 medium red onion, chopped
- 2 garlic cloves, minced
- 1 (15 oz) can diced tomatoes, without juice
- ½ tablespoons white wine vinegar
- 1 cup cooked quinoa
- Salt and black pepper to taste
- 1 tablespoon chopped fresh basil + extra for garnish
- 1 cup grated Monterey Jack cheese
- 4 large bell peppers, halved lengthways with stems and deseeded

ooooooooooooooooooooooooooooooooo

How to Cook:

1. Preheat oven to 350 F and line a baking tray with greaseproof paper.

2. Heat olive oil in a skillet and brown turkey for 10 to 12 minutes or until brown while stirring occasionally and breaking any lumps. Stir in onion and garlic; cook for 3 minutes or until onion is tender. Mix in tomatoes and cook for 10 minutes.

3. Stir in vinegar, quinoa, salt, black pepper, basil, and simmer for 1 to 2 minutes. Turn heat off.

4. Sit bell peppers on baking tray, fill with turkey mixture, and top with Monterey Jack cheese. Bake in oven for 20 to 35 minutes or until bell peppers soften.

5. Remove peppers, garnish with basil and serve warm.

(4) Unstuffed Turkey Bell Peppers

A quick fix to enjoy with rice, pasta, or bread.

Makes: 4

Preparation Time: 10 mins

Cooking Time: 25 mins

Ingredient List:

- 1 tablespoon olive oil
- 1 lb. ground turkey
- Salt and black pepper to taste
- 1 each orange and yellow bell pepper, deseeded and chopped
- 1 medium onion, chopped
- 2 garlic cloves, minced
- 1 (28 oz) can crushed tomatoes
- 1 (14.5 oz) can chopped tomatoes
- 1 teaspoon dried oregano
- 1 teaspoon dried basil
- 1 ½ cups chicken broth
- 1 cup grated cheddar cheese for topping
- Chopped fresh basil for garnish

ooooooooooooooooooooooooooooooooo

How to Cook:

1. Heat olive oil in a large skillet and cook turkey for 10 minutes or till brown; season with salt and black pepper.

2. Mix in bell peppers, onion, garlic, and cook for 5 minutes or till tender. Stir both types of tomatoes, oregano, basil, chicken broth, and season with salt and black pepper. Cover, bring to a boil, and simmer for 10 to 15 minutes or till liquid reduces by half.

3. Dish food, top with cheddar cheese, basil, and serve warm with rice.

(5) Pork, Brown Rice and Olives Stuffed Peppers

What a loaded treat we have here! I love to serve this dish for Saturday dinner because it settles the busy week with so much heartiness.

Makes: 4

Preparation Time: 10 mins

Cooking Time: 60 mins

Ingredient List:

- 1 tablespoon olive oil
- 1 lb. ground pork
- 1 medium brown onion, chopped
- 2 garlic cloves, minced
- 1 (15 oz) can chopped fire-roasted tomatoes
- ½ lemon, juiced
- 1 cup cooked brown rice
- Salt and black pepper to taste
- 1 tablespoon chopped fresh oregano + extra for garnish
- ¼ cup sliced Kalamata olives
- 1 cup grated Parmesan cheese
- 4 large bell peppers, halved lengthways with stems and deseeded

oooooooooooooooooooooooooooooooo

How to Cook:

1. Preheat oven to 350 F and grease a baking dish with cooking spray

2. Heat olive oil in a skillet and brown pork for 10 minutes while stirring occasionally and breaking any lumps. Stir in onion and garlic; cook for 3 minutes or until onion is tender. Mix in tomatoes and cook for 10 minutes.

3. Stir in lemon juice, rice, salt, black pepper, oregano, olives, and simmer for 1 to 2 minutes. Turn heat off.

4. Sit bell peppers in baking dish, fill with pork mixture, and top with Parmesan cheese. Bake in oven for 20 to 35 minutes or until bell peppers soften.

5. Remove peppers, garnish with oregano and serve warm.

(6) Roasted Pepper Salad with Balsamic Vinaigrette

A quick, easy assemble and toss salad you'll love for lunch.

Makes: 4

Preparation Time: 10 mins

Cooking Time: 25 mins

Ingredient List:

- 6 large bell peppers, mixed colors, seeds removed and cut into chunks
- 2 tablespoons olive oil
- Salt and black pepper to taste
- 1 ½ tablespoons balsamic vinegar
- 1 ½ teaspoons dried oregano
- 1 teaspoon garlic powder
- ¼ teaspoons red chili flakes
- ½ cup crumbled feta cheese
- 1/3 cup pitted black olives
- ¼ cup toasted pine nuts
- ¼ cup fresh basil leaves

ooooooooooooooooooooooooooooooo

How to Cook:

1. Preheat oven to 350 degrees F.

2. Spread bell peppers on a baking tray, drizzle with olive oil, and season with salt and black pepper; toss well and roast in oven for 20 to 25 minutes or until tender and lightly charred.

3. Meanwhile, whisk balsamic vinegar, oregano, garlic powder, and red chili flakes in a bowl.

4. Transfer peppers to a bowl when ready and drizzle with balsamic vinaigrette to taste; toss well.

5. Dish salad and top with feta cheese, olives, pine nuts, and basil. Serve immediately.

(7) Sweet Pepper, Onion, and Mushroom Medley

Make a pretty presentation at the table with this platter and whet appetites.

Makes: 4

Preparation Time: 10 mins

Cooking Time: 7 mins

Ingredient List:

- 1 tablespoon vegetable oil
- 2 large red bell peppers, seeds removed and sliced
- 1 large orange bell peppers, seeds removed and sliced
- 1 large yellow bell peppers, seeds removed and sliced
- 1 cup sliced cremini mushrooms
- 1 large yellow onion, sliced
- 1 garlic clove, minced
- Salt and black pepper to taste
- ¼ teaspoons dried basil
- 1 ½ tablespoons balsamic vinegar
- Chopped fresh parsley for garnish

ooooooooooooooooooooooooooooooooo

How to Cook:

1. Heat olive oil in a large skillet over medium heat and sauté mushrooms, bell peppers, and onion for 5 minutes or until tender. Mix in garlic and cook for 1 minute or until fragrant.

2. Season with salt, black pepper, basil, and vinegar; toss well and simmer for 1 minute.

3. Dish food, garnish with parsley, and serve warm.

(8) Cajun Chicken and Bell Pepper Bake

Spicy and creamy Cajun chicken as a one-pan dinner topped with sweet peppers for an appropriate low-carb serving.

Makes: 4

Preparation Time: 10 mins

Cooking Time: 33 mins

Ingredient List:

- 6 mini sweet peppers, seeds removed and sliced (red and yellow)
- 4 small chicken breasts, skinless and boneless
- Salt and black pepper to taste
- 1 ½ teaspoons Cajun seasoning
- 4 garlic cloves, minced
- 6 oz cream cheese, cold, and sliced into 8 slices
- ½ cup grated cheddar cheese

ooooooooooooooooooooooooooooooooo

How to Cook:

1. Preheat oven to 375 degrees F and grease a baking dish with cooking spray.

2. Spread half of bell peppers on bottom of baking dish –season chicken with salt, black pepper, and Cajun seasoning. Set chicken on peppers in a single layer and cover with remaining peppers.

3. Top with cream cheese, cheddar cheese, and bake in oven for 20 to 30 minutes or until chicken cooks through. Broil after for 2 to 3 minutes or until golden brown.

4. Dish food and serve warm.

(9) Bell Pepper Eggs

A lovely breakfast treat to add so much flavor into your day – it is a good mood booster.

Makes: 4

Preparation Time: 10 mins

Cooking Time: 12 mins

Ingredient List:

- 4 large mixed bell peppers, head sliced off and deseeded
- 1 tablespoon olive oil for drizzling
- Salt and black pepper to taste
- 4 eggs
- ½ teaspoons dried parsley
- ½ cup grated cheddar cheese, optional

oooooooooooooooooooooooooooooooo

How to Cook:

1. Preheat oven to 350 degrees F.

2. Sit bell peppers in a cast-iron pan or baking dish, drizzle with olive oil, and season with salt and black pepper.

3. Crack an egg into each bell pepper, season with salt, black pepper, and divide parsley and cheddar cheese on top.

4. Bake in oven for 10 to 12 minutes or until eggs whites set, yolk still runny, and bell peppers are tender.

5. Remove peppers onto a plate and serve warm.

(10) Peppers with Gnocchi and Sausage

Who knew gnocchi and peppers would pair so excellently like this? This recipe is giving us weekend chills.

Makes: 4

Preparation Time: 10 mins

Cooking Time: 18 mins

Ingredient List:

- 2 tablespoons olive oil
- ½ lb. ground Italian chicken sausage
- ½ medium white onion, finely chopped
- ½ each of green, red, and yellow bell pepper, sliced and chopped
- 2 (12 oz) packs gnocchi
- 24 oz prepared marinara sauce with garlic
- Salt and black pepper to taste
- Grated Parmesan cheese for topping
- Chopped fresh basil for topping

ooooooooooooooooooooooooooooooooo

How to Cook:

1. Heat olive oil in a skillet over medium heat and brown sausage for 10 minutes.

2. Stir in onion, peppers, gnocchi, and cook for 3 minutes or until sweaty. Mix in marinara sauce, season with salt, black pepper, and simmer for 4 to 5 minutes or until gnocchi cooks.

3. Dish food, top with Parmesan cheese, basil, and serve warm.

(11) Gemelli in Roasted Pepper Sauce

When the hunger pangs are crying aloud, quickly put this dish together, and calm them.

Makes: 4

Preparation Time: 10 mins

Cooking Time: 16 mins

Ingredient List:

- 1 tablespoon olive oil
- 1 medium onion, chopped
- 1 garlic clove, minced
- 4 large tomatoes, chopped
- 2 roasted red bell peppers, chopped
- ¼ cup vegetable broth
- 1 tablespoon balsamic vinegar
- 1 ½ cups cooked gemelli
- Grated Parmesan cheese for topping

ooooooooooooooooooooooooooooooooo

How to Cook:

1. Heat olive oil in a medium pot and cook onion and garlic for 3 minutes or until tender.

2. Stir in tomatoes, bell pepper, broth, and season with salt and black pepper. Cover, bring to a boil and simmer for 10 minutes or until sauce reduces by a third.

3. Stir in balsamic vinegar, gemelli, and simmer for 2 to 3 minutes to warm pasta; adjust taste with salt and black pepper.

4. Dish food, top with Parmesan cheese and serve warm.

(12) Buttered Steak with Peppers and Green Beans

Making dinner in a rush can still taste good. This recipe is one that will be ready in no time yet bursting with sweet flavors.

Makes: 2

Preparation Time: 10 mins

Cooking Time: 21 mins

Ingredient List:

- 1 tablespoon olive oil
- 2 (1-inch thick) boneless beef steaks, trimmed
- Salt and black pepper to taste
- 1 teaspoon garlic powder
- 3 tablespoons salted butter
- 1 cup mini peppers, seeds removed and sliced
- 1 cup green beans, trimmed
- 1 onion, thinly sliced
- 2 teaspoons fresh thyme leaves
- 1 lemon, juiced
- 1 tablespoon chopped fresh parsley for garnish

oooooooooooooooooooooooooooooooo

How to Cook:

1. Heat 1 tablespoon of olive oil in a skillet, season beef on both sides with salt, black pepper, garlic powder, and cook in oil on both sides for 10 to 12 minutes or until cooked through to your desired doneness. Melt in 1 tablespoon of butter, spoon butter over beef, and put meats aside on serving plates.

2. Melt remaining butter in another skillet and sauté peppers, green beans, and onions for 5 to 7 minutes or until tender. Stir in thyme, cook for 1 minute, or until fragrant. Add lemon juice and simmer for 1 minute, season with salt.

3. Dish beef with vegetables, garnish with parsley and serve warm.

(13) Chicken Fajita Peppers

Make fajita chicken for yourself and indulge all alone. This recipe makes you assemble it quickly without the stress involved for bigger servings.

Makes: 2

Preparation Time: 10 mins

Cooking Time: 40 mins

Ingredient List:

- 1 tablespoon vegetable oil
- 1 chicken breasts, boneless and skinless
- Salt and black pepper to taste
- 1 small white onion, sliced
- 2 garlic cloves, minced
- 2 teaspoons fajita seasoning
- ¼ cup cooked rice
- 1 tablespoon chopped fresh cilantro
- 1 teaspoon fresh lime juice
- 1 large green bell pepper, halved lengthways and deseeded
- ½ cup grated cheddar cheese
- Sour cream for serving
- Pico de gallo for serving

oooooooooooooooooooooooooooooooo

How to Cook:

1. Preheat oven to 350 degrees F and grease a baking dish with cooking spray.

2. Heat olive oil in a skillet, season chicken with salt, black pepper, and cook chicken in oil on both sides for 10 minutes or until cooked through. Put chicken on a plate, shred with a fork, and set aside.

3. Add onion and garlic to skillet and sweat for 3 minutes. Return chicken to skillet and add fajita seasoning, rice, cilantro, and lime juice; simmer for 1 to 2 minutes and turn heat off.

4. Divide chicken mixture into bell pepper halves, top with cheddar cheese, and sit peppers in baking dish. Bake for 20 to 25 minutes or until peppers are tender.

5. Remove peppers onto a serving platter, top with sour cream, pico de gallo, and serve warm.

(14) Chicken and Pepper Fusilli

It's a colorful and inviting summer dish yet easy to assemble and it tastes terrific too.

Makes: 4

Preparation Time: 10 mins

Cooking Time: 19 mins

Ingredient List:

- 8 oz uncooked fusilli
- 3 tablespoons olive oil
- 4 boneless and skinless chicken breasts, cut into bite-size strips
- Salt and black pepper to taste
- 1 medium red bell pepper, seeds removed and sliced
- 1 medium orange bell pepper, seeds removed and sliced
- 1 medium yellow bell pepper, seeds removed and sliced
- 2 large carrots, peeled and sliced
- 1 zucchini, chopped
- 4 garlic cloves, minced
- 4 tablespoons chicken broth, plus more if necessary
- ¼ cup chopped fresh basil
- 1 teaspoon chopped fresh oregano
- ¾ grated Parmesan cheese

ooooooooooooooooooooooooooooooooo

How to Cook:

1. Cook fusilli according to the package instructions until al dente; drain and set aside.

2. Heat 1 tablespoon of olive oil in a large skillet, season chicken with salt, black pepper, and cook in oil for 10 minutes or until done. Transfer to a plate and set aside.

3. Heat remaining olive oil in skillet and sauté bell pepper, carrots, and zucchini for 4 minutes or until tender. Stir in garlic and cook for 1 minute or until fragrant.

4. Add chicken and fusilli to skillet with chicken broth. Season with basil, oregano, and simmer for 2 to 3 minutes or until well warmed through. Mix in Parmesan cheese and let melt for a minute.

5. Dish food and serve warm.

(15) Italian Orzo Stuffed Bell Peppers

A hearty Italian pasta composition that is excellent for dinner.

Makes: 4

Preparation Time: 10 mins

Cooking Time: 60 mins

Ingredient List:

- 1 tablespoon olive oil
- 1 lb. ground beef
- 1 medium yellow onion, chopped
- 2 garlic cloves, minced
- 1 (15 oz) can pasta sauce
- ½ tablespoons Italian seasoning
- 1 cup cooked orzo
- Salt and black pepper to taste
- 1 tablespoon chopped fresh basil + extra for garnish
- 4 large red bell peppers, halved lengthways and seeds removed
- 1 cup grated Parmesan cheese for topping

oooooooooooooooooooooooooooooooooo

How to Cook:

1. Preheat oven to 350 F and line a baking tray with greaseproof paper.

2. Heat olive oil in a skillet and cook beef for 10 minutes or until brown while stirring occasionally and breaking any lumps. Stir in onion and garlic; cook for 3 minutes or until onion is tender. Mix in pasta sauce, Italian seasoning, and cook for 10 minutes.

3. Stir in orzo salt, black pepper, and simmer for 1 to 2 minutes. Turn heat off.

4. Sit bell peppers in baking dish, fill with beef mixture, and sprinkle with Parmesan cheese. Bake in oven for 20 to 35 minutes or until bell peppers soften.

5. Remove peppers, garnish with basil and serve warm.

(16) Bell Pepper Nachos

A smart dish for keto dieters; this recipe replaces tortilla chips with bell peppers for not only a health-conscious meal but also a more aromatic one.

Makes: 4

Preparation Time: 10 mins

Cooking Time: 15 mins

Ingredient List:

- 1 lb. baby bell peppers, halved and deseeded
- 1 lb. chorizo, cooked and drained
- 2 cups Mexican Cheese
- ½ cup chopped green onions
- ¼ cup chopped fresh cilantro
- ¼ cup thinly sliced radishes
- 4 tablespoons Cotija cheese

ooooooooooooooooooooooooooooooooo

How to Cook:

1. Preheat oven to 350 degrees F and grease a casserole dish with cooking spray.

2. Make two layers of all the ingredients in the dish - arrange bell peppers in dish with open side facing up and top with remaining ingredients.

3. Bake in oven for 10 to 15 minutes or until cheese melts.

4. Remove casserole dish and serve warm.

(17) Lamb and Goat Cheese Stuffed Peppers

If you are crazy about lamb like me, then you'll be splurging on this dish for days. I like to make enough to enjoy as an overnight serving – it tastes better the next day.

Makes: 4

Preparation Time: 10 mins

Cooking Time: 64 mins

Ingredient List:

- 1 tablespoon olive oil
- 1 lb. ground lamb
- 1 medium carrot, chopped
- 3 cremini mushrooms, chopped
- 1 medium red onion, chopped
- 2 garlic cloves, minced
- 1 (15 oz) can diced tomatoes, without juice
- 1 cup cooked rice
- Salt and black pepper to taste
- 1 tablespoon chopped fresh parsley
- 4 large bell peppers, top sliced off, seeds removed, and top remained
- 1 cup crumbled goat cheese for topping

ooooooooooooooooooooooooooooooooo

How to Cook:

1. Preheat oven to 350 F and line a baking tray with greaseproof paper.

2. Heat olive oil in a skillet and brown lamb for 10 to 12 minutes while stirring occasionally and breaking any lumps. Stir in carrots, mushrooms, onion, and garlic; cook for 5 minutes or until onion is tender. Mix in tomatoes and cook for 10 minutes.

3. Stir in rice, salt, black pepper, parsley, and simmer for 1 to 2 minutes. Turn heat off.

4. Sit bell peppers on baking tray, fill with lamb mixture, top with goat cheese, and place pepper caps on top. Bake in oven for 20 to 35 minutes or until bell peppers soften.

5. Remove peppers and serve warm.

(18) Bell Pepper, Zucchini, and Snap Pea Stir-Fry

In thirty minutes, lunch is ready, which is a fantastic serving for summer. Also, check out how walnuts blend well with sweet peppers.

Makes: 4

Preparation Time: 10 mins

Cooking Time: 9 mins

Ingredient List:

For sauce:

- ¼ cup low-sodium soy sauce or tamari
- 1 tablespoon rice vinegar
- 2 tablespoons hoisin sauce
- ¼ to ½ teaspoons red pepper flakes
- 1 teaspoon grated fresh ginger
- 2 garlic cloves, minced
- 1 teaspoon orange zest
- 1 ½ tablespoons orange juice
- 2 teaspoons cornstarch

For stir-fry:

- 2 tablespoons olive oil
- 1 medium onion, sliced
- 1 medium red bell pepper, seeds removed and sliced
- 2 cups snap peas, trimmed
- 1 medium zucchini, chopped
- ½ cup raw walnuts, chopped
- 1 (15 oz) can chickpeas, drained and rinsed
- ¼ cup chopped fresh basil

ooooooooooooooooooooooooooooooooooo

How to Cook:

1. Combine all sauce ingredients in a bowl and set aside.

2. Heat olive oil in a skillet and stir-fry onion, bell pepper, snap peas, and zucchini for 3 minutes or until tender.

3. Mix in sauce and simmer for 2 to 3 minutes. Stir in walnuts, chickpeas, and let warm through for 2 to 3 minutes; adjust taste with salt as needed and mix in basil.

4. Dish stir-fry and serve with rice.

(19) Filet Mignon with Tarragon Peppers

An easy romantic gesture that is perfect for date night. Enjoy the sweetness that comes from soft meat pieces and flavorful peppers.

Makes: 2

Preparation Time: 20 mins

Cooking Time: 29 mins

Ingredient List:

For filet mignon:

- 1 tablespoon vegetable oil
- 1 teaspoon chopped fresh thyme
- 2 (1 ½ inch-thick) filet mignon steaks
- 1 large shallot, minced
- ¼ cup red wine
- ½ teaspoons cornstarch
- ¾ cup beef broth
- Salt and black pepper to taste

For tarragon peppers:

- 1 tablespoon olive oil
- 4 cups sliced mixed bell peppers
- 1 small red onion, sliced
- 2 scallions, sliced
- ½ teaspoons chopped fresh tarragon
- Salt to taste

OOOOOOOOOOOOOOOOOOOOOOOOOOOOOOOOOO

How to Cook:

For filet mignon:

1. Preheat oven to 400 degrees F.

2. Heat olive oil in a cast-iron skillet over medium heat. Season steak on all sides with salt, black pepper, and half of thyme. Sear steak in pan for 2 minutes per side or until brown crust forms and transfer skillet to oven. Cook for 10 minutes for medium. Transfer steak to a plate, cover with foil, and set aside for serving.

3. Return skillet to heat and sauté shallots for 3 minutes or until tender. Stir in remaining thyme; cook for 1 minute or until fragrant. Pour in red wine, beef broth, stir and cook for 6 minutes. Mix in cornstarch and cook for 2 to 3 minutes or until sauce thickens. Adjust taste with salt and black pepper. Turn heat off.

For tarragon peppers:

4. Heat olive oil in a skillet and sauté bell peppers and onion for 5 minutes or until tender; season with salt.

5. Dish beef, peppers, and serve warm with sauce.

(20) Rice and Chicken Stuffed Peppers

Gather rice and chicken stew into one whole and enjoy the juicy, flavor-packed bites.

Makes: 4

Preparation Time: 10 mins

Cooking Time: 62 mins

Ingredient List:

- 1 tablespoon olive oil
- 1 lb. ground chicken
- 1 medium carrot, chopped
- 1 medium red onion, chopped
- 2 garlic cloves, minced
- 1 (15 oz) can diced tomatoes, without juice
- ½ tablespoons fresh lemon juice
- 1 cup cooked rice
- Salt and black pepper to taste
- 1 tablespoon chopped fresh basil + extra for garnish
- 4 large bell peppers, top sliced off, seeds removed, and top remained

ooooooooooooooooooooooooooooooooo

How to Cook:

1. Preheat oven to 350 F and line a baking tray with greaseproof paper.

2. Heat olive oil in a skillet and brown chicken for 10 minutes or until brown while stirring occasionally and breaking any lumps. Stir in carrots, onion, and garlic; cook for 5 minutes or until onion is tender. Mix in tomatoes and cook for 10 minutes.

3. Stir in lemon juice, rice, salt, black pepper, basil, and simmer for 1 to 2 minutes. Turn heat off.

4. Sit bell peppers on baking tray, fill with chicken mixture, and place pepper caps on top. Bake in oven for 20 to 35 minutes or until bell peppers soften.

5. Remove peppers, garnish with basil and serve warm.

(21) Pesto Marinated Peppers

This simple dish is a great addition to other main meals like meats and grains. You can make it in advance and store it for up to a week in the refrigerator as you dig in gradually.

Makes: 4

Preparation Time: 10 mins

Cooking Time: 5 mins

Ingredient List:

- 1 ½ lb. mini sweet peppers, seeds removed
- ½ tablespoons olive oil
- 1 cup basil pesto
- 2 tablespoons garlic paste
- 6 tablespoons granulated sugar
- Salt to taste
- 1 ¼ cups plain vinegar

oooooooooooooooooooooooooooooooooo

How to Cook:

1. Preheat a grill pan over medium heat, toss bell peppers with olive oil, and grill for 5 minutes or until slightly charred and softened.

2. Put bell peppers in a bowl, add remaining ingredients and mix well.

3. Store bell pepper mixture in a Tupperware and preserve in the fridge for up to a week.

(22) Bell Pepper and Gorgonzola Bungalow

Such a quick combination yet a splurge! You will love every bite of this dish.

Makes: 4

Preparation Time: 10 mins

Cooking Time: 46 mins

Ingredient List:

- 1 tablespoon olive oil
- 1 lb. ground beef
- Salt and black pepper to taste
- ½ medium yellow onion, chopped
- 2 medium green bell peppers, seeds removed and chopped
- 2 garlic cloves, minced
- 1 cup white rice, cooked
- ¼ cup tomato paste
- 1 (14.5 oz) can chopped tomatoes, without liquid
- 2 tablespoons Worcestershire sauce
- ½ cup crumbled gorgonzola cheese
- ½ cup shredded mozzarella cheese

ooooooooooooooooooooooooooooooooo

How to Cook:

1. Preheat oven to 350 degrees F and set a baking dish aside.

2. Heat olive oil in a medium skillet and cook beef for 10 minutes or until brown. Add onion, bell peppers, and cook for 5 minutes or until tender. Stir in garlic and cook for 1 minute or until fragrant.

3. Mix in rice, tomato paste, tomatoes, Worcestershire sauce, and simmer for 5 minutes; adjust taste with salt and black pepper. Turn heat off and stir in gorgonzola cheese.

4. Transfer beef mixture to baking dish, scatter mozzarella cheese on top, and bake for 25 minutes or until cheese melts and is golden brown on top.

(23) Bell Pepper and Potato Ratatouille

An aroma haven of a ratatouille that you can't get enough of.

Makes: 4

Preparation Time: 15 mins

Cooking Time: 62 mins

Ingredient List:

- 3 medium potatoes, peeled
- 2 tablespoons olive oil + extra for drizzling
- 1 to 2 cups tomato basil sauce
- 2 garlic cloves, finely chopped
- ½ teaspoons red chili flakes
- 1 ½ tablespoons fresh thyme leaves
- Salt and black pepper to taste
- 1 eggplant, thinly sliced
- 1 large red bell pepper, seeds removed and thinly sliced
- 1 large green bell pepper, seeds removed and thinly sliced
- 1 large yellow bell pepper, seeds removed and thinly sliced
- 1 large zucchini, thinly sliced

OOOOOOOOOOOOOOOOOOOOOOOOOOOOOOOO

How to Cook:

1. Preheat oven to 375 degrees F.

2. Bring 2 ½ cups of salted water to a boil and cook in potatoes for 20 to 22 minutes or until tender. Drain and thinly slice potatoes.

3. Brush a round casserole dish with olive oil and spread tomato sauce at the bottom of the dish. Season with garlic, red chili flakes, thyme, salt, black pepper, and layer the bell peppers, potatoes, and zucchinis near to each other all around the casserole, as seen in the image; drizzle with some olive oil.

4. Cover dish with greaseproof paper and bake in oven for 30 to 40 minutes or until vegetables are tender.

5. Remove dish and serve warm.

(24) Mini Pizza Peppers

Are you craving pizza and can't bring yourself to make one? Have these pizza peppers to satisfy the desire.

Makes: 4

Preparation Time: 10 mins

Cooking Time: 15 mins

Ingredient List:

- Olive oil cooking spray
- 8 mini bell peppers, halved lengthways and seeds removed
- ¼ cup pizza sauce
- ½ cup grated mozzarella cheese

ooooooooooooooooooooooooooooooooo

How to Cook:

1. Preheat oven to 350 degrees F.

2. Grease a baking sheet with cooking spray and arrange peppers on top in a single layer and with open side open.

3. Spray peppers with cooking spray, divide pizza sauce into peppers, and top with mozzarella cheese. Bake in oven for 10 to 15 minutes or until cheese melts and peppers soften.

4. Serve warm.

(25) Sweet Potato and Pepper Soup

A catchy and easy soup to enjoy on a cold day or evening.

Makes: 4

Preparation Time: 10 mins

Cooking Time: 24 mins

Ingredient List:

- 1 tablespoon olive oil
- 1 large red bell pepper, seeds removed and sliced
- 1 medium yellow onion, chopped
- 3 garlic cloves, peeled and crushed
- 2 large sweet potatoes, peeled and chopped
- 4 cups vegetable broth
- 1 teaspoon smoked paprika + extra for topping
- ¼ teaspoons cayenne pepper or to taste
- 1 tablespoon fresh lemon juice
- Salt and black pepper to taste
- Sour cream for serving
- Chopped fresh scallions for garnish

ooooooooooooooooooooooooooooooooo

How to Cook:

1. Heat olive oil in a large pot and sauté bell pepper and onion for 3 minutes or until tender. Stir in garlic and cook for 1 minute or until fragrant.

2. Mix in sweet potatoes, vegetable broth, paprika, cayenne pepper, salt, and black pepper. Cover, bring to a boil, and simmer for 15 to 20 minutes or until potatoes are tender.

3. Puree soup with an immersion blender until smooth and stir in lemon juice; adjust taste with salt and pepper.

4. Dish soup, top with sour cream, paprika, scallions, and serve warm.

(26) Curried Peppers and Potatoes

We are getting Indian vibes from this dish, which is an easy way to introduce something new to the table for a flair.

Makes: 4

Preparation Time: 15 mins

Cooking Time: 29 mins

Ingredient List:

- 3 tablespoons vegetable oil
- 1 teaspoon whole cumin seeds
- 4 medium green bell peppers, seeds removed and cut into chunks
- 1 medium onion, chopped
- 3 garlic cloves, minced
- 2 medium tomatoes, chopped
- 3 medium potatoes, peeled and chopped
- 2 teaspoons cumin and coriander powder
- 1 teaspoon cayenne pepper
- ½ teaspoons curry powder
- 2/3 cup vegetable broth
- Salt to taste
- Chopped fresh cilantro for garnish
- 1 lime, sliced for garnish

ooooooooooooooooooooooooooooooooo

How to Cook:

1. Heat oil in medium pot and toast cumin seeds for 1 minute. Stir in bell pepper, onion, garlic, and cook for 3 minutes or until sweaty.

2. Mix in tomatoes, potatoes, cumin and coriander powder, cayenne pepper, curry powder, vegetable broth, and salt. Cover, bring to a boil, and then simmer for 20 to 25 minutes or until potatoes are fork-tender and liquid absorbed.

3. Dish food, garnish with cilantro, and serve with lime slices.

(27) Greek Stuffed Peppers

Are you a beginner cook? These peppers are an easy way to make a satisfying dinner without sweating it.

Makes: 4

Preparation Time: 10 mins

Cooking Time: 60 mins

Ingredient List:

- 1 tablespoon olive oil
- 1 lb. ground beef
- 1 medium red onion, chopped
- 2 garlic cloves, minced
- 1 (15 oz) can chopped fire-roasted tomatoes
- ½ lemon, juiced
- 1 cup cooked rice
- Salt and black pepper to taste
- 1 tablespoon chopped fresh oregano + extra for garnish
- 1 cup crumbled feta cheese
- 4 large bell peppers, halved lengthways with stems and deseeded

ooooooooooooooooooooooooooooooooo

How to Cook:

1. Preheat oven to 350 F and line a baking tray with greaseproof paper.

2. Heat olive oil in a skillet and brown beef for 10 minutes while stirring occasionally and breaking any lumps. Stir in onion and garlic; cook for 3 minutes or until onion is tender. Mix in tomatoes and cook for 10 minutes.

3. Stir in lemon juice, rice, salt, black pepper, oregano, and simmer for 1 to 2 minutes. Turn heat off.

4. Sit bell peppers on baking tray, fill with rice and meat mixture, and top with feta cheese. Bake in oven for 20 to 35 minutes or until bell peppers soften.

5. Remove peppers, garnish with oregano and serve warm.

(28) Cajun Chicken Spaghetti with Peppers

It bursts with so much color, flavor, and taste that you will love so much.

Makes: 2

Preparation Time: 10 mins

Cooking Time: 30 mins

Ingredient List:

- 6 oz dried spaghetti
- 1 tablespoon olive oil
- 2 chicken breasts, skinless and boneless
- 1 tablespoon Cajun seasoning
- Salt and black pepper to taste
- 4 tablespoons unsalted butter
- 1 medium red bell pepper, seeds removed and thinly sliced
- 1 medium green bell pepper, seeds removed and thinly sliced
- 2 scallions, sliced + extra for garnish
- 1 ½ cups heavy cream
- ¼ teaspoons dried basil
- ¼ teaspoons lemon pepper
- ¼ teaspoons garlic powder

oooooooooooooooooooooooooooooooooo

How to Cook:

1. Cook spaghetti according to package's instruction until al dente, about 10 to 12 minutes. Drain and set aside.

2. Meanwhile, heat olive oil in a skillet, season chicken with Cajun seasoning, salt, black pepper, and cook in oil on both sides for 8 to 10 minutes or until chicken is golden brown and cooked through. Transfer chicken to a plate, slice into pieces, and set aside.

3. Melt butter in skillet and sauté bell peppers and scallions for 5 minutes or until tender. Spoon vegetables to side of chicken and set aside.

4. Pour heavy cream into skillet, season with basil, lemon pepper, garlic powder, salt, black pepper, and simmer for 1 minute. Fold in spaghetti, chicken, and vegetables; simmer for 1 to 2 minutes or until chicken warms through.

5. Dish food, garnish with scallions and serve warm.

(29) Herb Sautéed Green Peppers

Add more flavor to your platter with this simple side dish, which works fantastic with meat servings.

Makes: 4

Preparation Time: 10 mins

Cooking Time: 32 mins

Ingredient List:

- 2 tablespoons olive oil
- 4 large green bell peppers, seeds removed and sliced
- ½ medium red onion, sliced
- 2 tablespoons chopped fresh parsley
- 1 teaspoon dried oregano
- 1 tablespoon red wine vinegar
- Salt and black pepper to taste

ooooooooooooooooooooooooooooooooo

How to Cook:

1. Heat olive oil in medium skillet and sauté bell peppers and onion for 3 minutes or until sweaty.

2. Stir in parsley, oregano, red wine vinegar, salt, and black pepper, simmer for 2 minutes or until flavors combine well.

3. Dish food and serve warm.

(30) Peperonata

A unique Italian stew dedicated to using mainly bell peppers for serving rice, pasta, and other types of grains.

Makes: 4

Preparation Time: 10 mins

Cooking Time: 38 mins

Ingredient List:

- ¾ cup olive oil, divided
- 2 medium yellow onions, sliced with ¼-inch thick
- 4 lb. red, yellow, and orange bell peppers (about 6 large bell peppers), seeds removed and sliced
- 6 garlic cloves, thinly sliced
- 1 cup tomato paste
- 2 sprigs basil, leaves extracted
- Salt to taste
- 1 tablespoon red or white wine vinegar

oooooooooooooooooooooooooooooooooo

How to Cook:

1. Heat half of olive oil in a large pot over medium heat and sauté onions and bell peppers for 7 minutes or until tender. Stir in garlic and cook for 1 minute or until fragrant.

2. Mix in tomato paste, basil, salt, and remaining olive oil. Simmer for 30 minutes or until peppers are very soft.

3. Stir in vinegar and serve warm.

Afterthought

Do you have any comments about my book? It's been an overwhelmingly long month putting together this book, and your opinion would make me glad. Also, many people are seeking the right book, and your feedback is vital in helping me know how to be better and guiding others to the perfect book.

Thank you,

Keanu Wood

Biography

The food industry looked like the perfect place to showcase his love for food, coming from the fashion industry. We would like to say that he did not make a mistake as he immediately made his mark as a fine dining restaurant extraordinaire.

Being an Asian-American also made customers fall in love with his dishes, as Keanu carefully combined these two cultures, cuisines, ingredients, flavors, and cooking styles to deliver mouth-watering and rich, decadent food for everyone.

Will Cook learn how to mix flavors to invoke taste, and using the Yin and Yang symbol, his business balanced food with impeccable precision. While customers loved the décor, ambiance, and good service, it was the food that made all the difference.

He moved back to his hometown to bring his talent, skills, and diverse food to a new palate. His uncanny mastery of organization and putting that extra effort

Printed in Great Britain
by Amazon